Dear Reader,

We all need our own little BLUEPRINTS, or plans, in life. Sometimes making a plan is fun. Sometimes it's hard. Sometimes the plan doesn't work, so we make a new one. And sometimes, the plan is exactly what we need, just when we need it. As you read this Have a Plan Book, we hope you will ask questions, talk about it with family and friends, and create your very own plan. You can do this on your own or together with a grown-up.

Your plan may grow and change each time you read your book, and that's great! As life happens, plans change. But remember, having a little Blueprint is always helpful, in difficult times and in good times. So go ahead: BLUEPRINT IT!

Lovingly,

Your friends at little BLUEPRINT

P.S. Children and adults around the world are making their own little BLUEPRINTS. If you want to see the plans of others, or share yours, just go to

www.littleBLUEPRINT.com

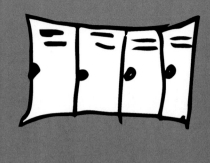

## HAVE A PLAN *Books*

To purchase a hardcover or
personalized version of any
little BLUEPRINT book,
with names, optional photo(s),
and details, please go to:

www.littleBLUEPRINT.com

The author would like to thank,
for all of their support and expertise:
Dan Siegel, M.D.;
Nina Shapiro, M.D.;
Pattie Fitzgerald
(Founder, Safely Ever After, Inc., www.safelyeverafter.com); and
my editors, Leslie Budnick and Gina Shaw.
A special thanks to:
Phoebe, age 10, for her blueprint illustration; and
Brooke, age 10, for her title page illustration.

# TO KEEP
## My Body Safe,
## I HAVE A PLAN

by Katherine Eskovitz

*illustrated by* Jessica Churchill

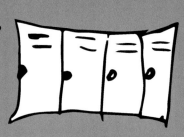

I know how to keep my body safe.

WHEN I WAS A BABY, my parents were in charge of keeping my body safe. They washed my body, changed my diapers, and fed me food.

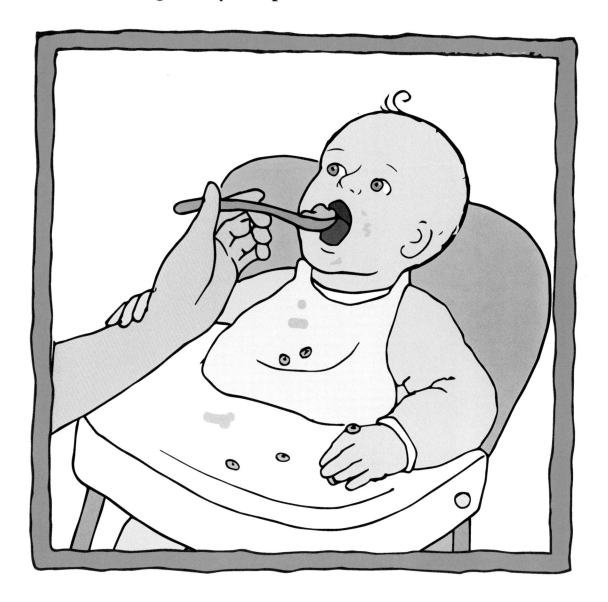

Now that I am older, I AM MORE INDEPENDENT.
I do more things on my own:
I go to school, I go to my own activities, and I go on play dates.

Keeping my body **SAFE**
wherever I am means
that I am not in danger,
and I do not get hurt.

When I am busy during the day,

it is important to be a SAFE KID

and to make sure my friends are safe, too.

SAFE ADULTS are people my parents and I trust.
They do not make me uncomfortable, and
they always follow safety rules to help keep me safe.

I can keep my body safe by following some simple safety rules that all SAFE KIDS and SAFE ADULTS should follow.

A very easy and important safety rule is that the parts of my body that I cover with a bathing suit are

PRIVATE.

# Of course, when I take a bath or a shower,

I wash my entire body to keep it CLEAN and HEALTHY.

A parent or SAFE ADULT may help younger
children wash their bodies.

When I go to the DOCTOR'S OFFICE
for a check-up, or if I am sick,
the doctor may examine my whole body.
A safe adult is always with me
at the Doctor's office.

But the important rule to always remember is
that the PRIVATE areas
of my body are PRIVATE.
They should not be touched or looked at
by other people:

NOT BY STRANGERS,
NOT BY TEACHERS,
NOT BY COACHES,
NOT BY NEIGHBORS,
NOT BY MY PARENTS' FRIENDS,
NOT BY MY COUSINS,
AND NOT BY BIG KIDS.

I am the BOSS OF MY BODY.

My body belongs to me,
and I am in charge of it.

BE SAFE: KEEP MY PRIVATE AREAS PRIVATE.

# Hugs can be great, especially from someone I love.

But if I do not want to be touched,

**IT IS ALWAYS OKAY TO SAY NO.**

It's not rude to say no to a touch because my feelings about my body are important. A **SAFE ADULT** will listen to me if I do not want to be touched.

BE SAFE: ALWAYS SAY "NO" IF I DO NOT FEEL LIKE BEING TOUCHED.

If anyone tries to look at or touch the private parts of my body, or asks me to touch theirs,

I should say "NO, STOP,"

as strong and loud as I want.

Then I should tell my parents or

a safe adult right away,

until I am sure I found

a safe adult who has heard me.

BE SAFE: IF SOMEONE TRIES TO LOOK AT OR TOUCH MY PRIVATE PARTS, OR ASKS ME TO TOUCH THEIRS, I WILL SAY NO. THEN I WILL TELL A SAFE ADULT UNTIL SOMEONE HEARS ME AND HELPS.

If someone says "DON'T TELL YOUR PARENTS,"
I should always TELL my parents immediately
because SAFE KIDS DO NOT KEEP SECRETS from their
parents, especially about touches.

When it comes to my body, I should always
TELL if someone says "DON'T TELL"–
EVEN IF SOMEONE IS ACTING SWEETLY,
OR GIVES ME PRESENTS,
OR IS JUST PLAYING A GAME,
EVEN IF I KNOW THAT PERSON WELL,

I do not keep secrets from my parents.

It is important that I tell a safe adult when
I think someone is not following the safety
rules, even if I am not sure.
IT IS NEVER MY FAULT
IF SOMEONE IS NOT ACTING SAFELY.

The best way to keep safe is to tell my parents or another safe adult because they can help me.

BE SAFE: IF SOMEONE SAYS DON'T TELL MY PARENTS, I WILL ALWAYS TELL MY PARENTS OR A SAFE ADULT RIGHT AWAY.

In addition to following safety rules,
we all have our very own safety protector
inside of us.
We have feelings that we can
listen to and trust to keep us safe.

These feelings are called our

# INTUITION.

My INTUITION tells me if I am
SCARED, UNSURE, or UNCOMFORTABLE.

My head or my stomach might hurt, my heart might

beat faster, or it might be hard to breathe. I might quietly

wonder or tell myself that something seems odd or wrong.

The safety protector inside of me is sending me
a clue that there might be DANGER.
My INTUITION is very smart.

I should pay attention to these clues because my feelings can protect me from danger.

If my INTUITION tells me something is not quite right

–I FEEL IT QUIETLY INSIDE OF ME–

I SHOULD ALWAYS TRUST THIS FEELING.

BE SAFE: LISTEN TO MY INTUTION TO HELP KEEP ME SAFE.

If my INTUITION tells me something is wrong,
I should tell a SAFE ADULT as soon as I can.
It is always safer to tell, even when I am
unsure, nervous, or embarrassed.

BE SAFE: IF MY INTUITION TELLS ME SOMETHING MIGHT BE WRONG,
TELL A SAFE ADULT AS SOON AS POSSIBLE.

One of the best parts about getting older is that
I CAN BE INDEPENDENT AND HAVE FUN
while staying SAFE by following safety rules.

I can help keep my body safe by making my own SAFETY PLAN, together with my family, using the ideas in this book.

Here are ideas I can use to make my own
**SAFETY PLAN.**

1. BE SAFE: KEEP MY PRIVATE AREAS PRIVATE.

2. BE SAFE: ALWAYS SAY "NO," IF I DO NOT WANT TO BE TOUCHED.

3. BE SAFE: IF SOMEONE TRIES TO LOOK AT OR TOUCH MY PRIVATE PARTS, OR ASKS ME TO TOUCH THEIRS, I WILL SAY NO. THEN I WILL TELL A SAFE ADULT UNTIL SOMEONE HEARS ME AND HELPS.

4. BE SAFE: IF SOMEONE SAYS DON'T TELL MY PARENTS, I SHOULD ALWAYS TELL MY PARENTS OR A SAFE ADULT RIGHT AWAY.

5. BE SAFE: LISTEN TO MY INTUITION TO HELP KEEP ME OUT OF DANGER.

6. BE SAFE: IF MY INTUITION TELLS ME SOMETHING MIGHT BE WRONG, TELL A SAFE ADULT AS SOON AS POSSIBLE.

# Here is MY PLAN

Other titles in the
# HAVE A PLAN Series

TO BE A HEALTHY EATER, I HAVE A PLAN

TO CELEBRATE THE HOLIDAYS, I HAVE A PLAN

WHEN I MISS SOMEONE SPECIAL, I HAVE A PLAN

WHEN I MISS MY SPECIAL PET, I HAVE A PLAN

TO BE SAFE AT HOME, I HAVE A PLAN

TO BE SAFE ON THE GO, I HAVE A PLAN

WHEN IT'S TIME FOR BED, I HAVE A PLAN

WHEN MY PARENTS DIVORCE, I HAVE A PLAN

WHEN MY PARENTS SEPARATE, I HAVE A PLAN

AND MORE

New titles added regularly at
www.littleBLUEPRINT.com

All titles are available ready-made and personalized

playground    School    Home

little
BLUEPRINT
Empowering children. Training the brain.
WWW.LITTLEBLUEPRINT.COM

Made in the USA
Middletown, DE
27 July 2017